Ad Libs for Adults 😄

Christmas Edition

JBC Story Press

Copyright ©2022. All rights reserved.

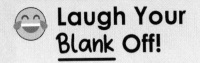

Laugh Your Blank Off!

Ad Libs for Adults
How to Play

Welcome! And get ready to *Laugh Your Blank Off!*

Number of players: 2-200+

There's really no limit… The more the merrier! This game is perfect for parties or just hanging out with friends. Players don't even have to be in the same room. Playing through video chat works great too.

Inside, you'll find 21 entertaining stories with blank spaces where words have been left out. Each story comes with a list of missing words of various types, e.g., ADJECTIVE, ADVERB, EXCLAMATION, NOUN, etc.

For each story, one player is the Story Teller. The Story Teller asks the other players to call out words to fill in the spaces of the story — WITHOUT first telling them what the story is about.

And bam! Just like that, you have a RIDICULOUSLY funny story!

The Story Teller reads the completed story out loud, and you all laugh so hard you almost pee your pants, cry, roll on the floor, or all of the above! *YOU* fill in the blank!

Adult Themes

This version of the game is for "grownups." That means stories may contain references to alcohol, romance, and other crazy adult stuff (you know, like work or parenting). Whether stories include "adult" language is up to you! Some groups like to use "spicy" swear words. Others prefer "sweet" and swear-free. It's your call!

One thing's for sure. Every story you create will be RIDICULOUSLY funny!

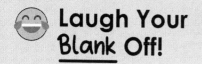

Laugh Your Blank Off!

Ad Libs for Adults How to Play

Examples

Before, with blanks:

"_____! We need to _____ to the party as
   EXCLAMATION   VERB

_____ as possible. We only have _____ minutes to get
ADVERB ENDING IN "LY"   NUMBER

there." So we jumped in the _____ car and sped off.
                                ADJECTIVE

After the Story Teller fills in the blanks with words from the players

"_____Yuck_____! We need to ____dance____ to the party as
   EXCLAMATION   VERB

____quietly_____ as possible. We only have __900__ minutes to get
ADVERB ENDING IN "LY"   NUMBER

there." So we jumped in the ___furry___ car and sped off.
                                ADJECTIVE

Quick Review

ADJECTIVE – Describes something or someone. Examples: Funny, huge, bossy, lame, fast.

ADVERB – Describes how something is done. You will only be asked for adverbs that end in "ly". Examples: Happily, badly, loudly.

NOUN or PLURAL NOUN – A person, place or thing. Examples: Singular – sister, restaurant, book. Plural – sisters, restaurants, books.

VERB, VERB ENDING IN "ING" or VERB (PAST TENSE) – Verbs are action words. Examples: Verb – Run, kiss, sing; Verb ending in "ing"– running, kissing, singing; Verb (past tense) – ran, kissed, sang

EXCLAMATION – A sound, word, or phrase that is spoken suddenly or loudly and expresses emotions, like excitement or anger, or shock or pain. Examples: "Oh no!", "Awesome!", "You're kidding me!", "Oof!"

OTHER – Specific words, like COLOR, ANIMAL, BODY PART, PLACE (like a city, state, country), or NAME OF FRIEND

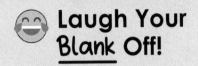

Laugh Your Blank Off!

"I Can't, I'm Watching Christmas Movies"

NUMBER
ADJECTIVE
MONTH
NOUN
ADJECTIVE
PLURAL NOUN
NOUN
NUMBER
PLURAL NOUN
ADJECTIVE
ADJECTIVE
VERB ENDING IN "ING"
NOUN
EXCLAMATION
NOUN
ADJECTIVE
ADJECTIVE

From *Laugh Your Blank Off! Christmas Edition* ©2022 JBC Story Press

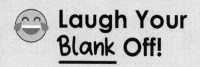

Laugh Your Blank Off!

"I Can't, I'm Watching Christmas Movies"

The TV screen is glowing, the lights are dimmed, I have _____ (NUMBER) bottle(s) of wine at hand and my _____ (ADJECTIVE) pajamas on. Every year, this is my perfect Christmas gift. I can't be the only person who starts getting excited in _____ (MONTH) about watching Christmas movies, right? Is it so bad that I pay extra for the _____ (NOUN) Channel so I can binge-watch _____ (ADJECTIVE) holiday movies and hide from my family and _____ (PLURAL NOUN) during this hectic season? I love my family more than _____ (NOUN). But every holiday season, I send the kids to spend _____ (NUMBER) days at their grandparents' and my husband to ski with his friends. No work, no carpool, no _____ (PLURAL NOUN). I spend the whole time watching _____ (ADJECTIVE) movies, ordering _____ (ADJECTIVE) take-out, baking cookies and _____ (VERB ENDING IN "ING") in my pajamas. One time, a _____ (NOUN) knocked out the electricity in our neighborhood. "_____ (EXCLAMATION)!" I shouted when the TV went black. But I quickly grabbed my cell phone and booked a room in a _____ (NOUN). The clerk looked _____ (ADJECTIVE) when I showed up wearing pajamas, but I was in my room watching movies faster than you can say "_____ (ADJECTIVE) Holidays!"

From *Laugh Your Blank Off! Christmas Edition* ©2022, JBC Story Press

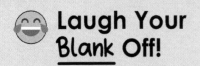

Laugh Your Blank Off!

5 Signs You Might Be On The Naughty List

ADJECTIVE
PLURAL NOUN
BODY PART (PLURAL)
NOUN
NOUN
PLURAL NOUN
VERB
VERB ENDING IN "ING"
PLURAL NOUN
NOUN
VERB
ADJECTIVE
VERB ENDING IN "ING"
NUMBER
EXCLAMATION

From *Laugh Your Blank Off! Christmas Edition* ©2022, JBC Story Press

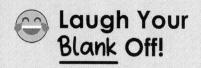

Laugh Your Blank Off!

5 Signs You Might Be On The Naughty List

Christmas is almost here! The house is _____. Holiday
                                          ADJECTIVE

_____ are playing. The feast is prepped. Now, you can
PLURAL NOUN

kick up your _____ and wait for Santa to deliver your
              BODY PART (PLURAL)

wishlist. Unless, that is, you're on The Naughty List. So, how do

you know if you're getting _____ in your stocking this
                               NOUN

year? Here's a list you'd better check twice…

1. Do you have Internet regret? Check your social media

_____. If you kept the naughty _____ to a
NOUN   PLURAL NOUN

minimum, you might _____ by.
                       VERB

2. Are you a grinch? If you start _____ about stores
                                    VERB ENDING IN "ING"

selling Christmas _____ in the summer, you might be
                   PLURAL NOUN

pushing your _____.
              NOUN

3. Are you egg-nogstic? – You don't have to actually

_____ this _____ drink, but take at least a sip
VERB   ADJECTIVE

each season.

4. Do you get tired of _____ to "All I Want for Christmas"
                         VERB ENDING IN "ING"

by Mariah Carey after only hearing it _____ times?
                                        NUMBER

If you answered "_____!" to any of these Naughty List "no
                  EXCLAMATION

nos," don't worry… there's always next year!

From *Laugh Your Blank Off! Christmas Edition* ©2022, JBC Story Press

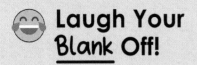

Laugh Your Blank Off!

Ugly Christmas Sweater Contest

NAME OF FRIEND 1
PLACE
VERB ENDING IN "ING"
PLURAL NOUN
BEVERAGE
FOOD
ADJECTIVE
ADJECTIVE
VERB
BODY PART (PLURAL)
PLURAL NOUN
ADJECTIVE
ADJECTIVE
PLURAL NOUN
PLURAL NOUN
PLURAL NOUN
NAME OF FRIEND 2
ANIMAL
NOUN
ADJECTIVE

From *Laugh Your Blank Off! Christmas Edition* ©2022, JBC Story Press

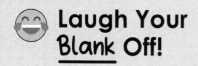

Ugly Christmas Sweater Contest

Every December, we gather at _____'s cabin in
                               NAME OF FRIEND 1
_____ to relax and celebrate the holidays. We spend a
       PLACE
few days _____, eating, and playing _____. We
         VERB ENDING IN "ING"   PLURAL NOUN
ski, drink spiked hot _____ in the jacuzzi, cook
                          BEVERAGE
_____ over the fire and listen to _____
       FOOD   ADJECTIVE
Christmas songs. After a few _____ cocktails, we like to
                                 ADJECTIVE
visit neighbors and _____ "Jingle Bells" at the top of our
                         VERB
_____. Not sure the neighbors like it as much as we do,
BODY PART (PLURAL)
but at least they don't throw _____ at us! The highlight of
                                  PLURAL NOUN
this _____ getaway, of course, is our "Ugly Christmas
      ADJECTIVE
Sweater" Contest. The competition is _____, so you have
                                         ADJECTIVE
to pull out all the _____! It's not unusual for sweaters to
                      PLURAL NOUN
have bells, _____, sequins, _____, ornaments,
             PLURAL NOUN   PLURAL NOUN
or all of the above! Last year, _____ surprised us when
                                  NAME OF FRIEND 2
she arrived at the cabin with a new pet _____!
                                           ANIMAL
She and her furry friend wore matching sweaters that read
"Happy PAW-lidays." They didn't win the top _____, but
                                                NOUN
they sure were _____!
                ADJECTIVE

From *Laugh Your Blank Off! Christmas Edition* ©2022, JBC Story Press

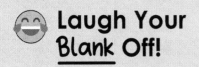

Laugh Your Blank Off!

A Christmas Prince, The Movie

NOUN
ADJECTIVE
ADVERB ENDING IN "LY"
ADJECTIVE
ADJECTIVE
ADJECTIVE
ADJECTIVE
VERB
ADJECTIVE
ADJECTIVE
NAME OF RESTAURANT
BODY PART
EMOTION
VERB
NOUN
EMOTION

From *Laugh Your Blank Off! Christmas Edition* ©2022, JBC Story Press

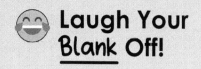

Laugh Your Blank Off!

A Christmas Prince, The Movie

After she finds her fiancé in _____ with his
                                    NOUN

_____ secretary, Megan thinks her life is over. She fills
ADJECTIVE

her days with work and thinks _____ about giving her
                              ADVERB ENDING IN "LY"

family the breakup news. Over drinks with her favorite coworker,

Ryan, Megan hatches a(n) _____ plan. She will simply
                         ADJECTIVE

find a replacement for her _____ ex-fiancé and bring him
                           ADJECTIVE

home for the holidays. Her new partner will be so charming that

her family will forget all about her _____ ex. Megan ropes
                                     ADJECTIVE

Ryan into helping. For Megan, the countdown to Christmas is a

blur of flirting and _____ dates. Megan can always count
                     ADJECTIVE

on Ryan, but when she asks for his help deciding which way to

_____ on Tinder, he gets _____ and leaves. On
VERB   ADJECTIVE

a particularly _____ date at _____ ,
               ADJECTIVE   NAME OF RESTAURANT

she gets sick to her _____. Instead of showing
                     BODY PART

_____, her date _____ while she is in the
EMOTION   VERB

restroom, sticking her with the check. Just as Megan starts to tear

up, Ryan arrives, carrying a bottle of _____ and some
                                       NOUN

tissues. Flooded with _____, Megan wonders if her
                      EMOTION

Christmas Prince has been at her side all along.

From *Laugh Your Blank Off! Christmas Edition* ©2022, JBC Story Press

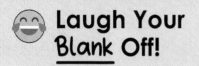

Laugh Your Blank Off!

Deck the Halls on a Dime

ADJECTIVE
NOUN
NOUN
NOUN
PLURAL NOUN
ADJECTIVE
PLURAL NOUN
ADJECTIVE
ADJECTIVE
ADJECTIVE
ADJECTIVE
ADJECTIVE
VERB
EXCLAMATION
NOUN
VERB ENDING IN "ING"
NUMBER
NUMBER

From *Laugh Your Blank Off! Christmas Edition* ©2022, JBC Story Press

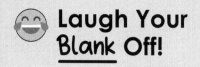

Laugh Your Blank Off!

Deck the Halls on a Dime

Do you love making your home look _____ for the
                                      ADJECTIVE
holidays, but hate spending a _____ to do it? We've got
                                      NOUN
you covered! Here are some creative _____-saving tips:
                                              NOUN

1. Get crafty! It's amazing what you can do with a glue gun, a little

_____ and some _____. Try making your own
   NOUN   PLURAL NOUN

_____ ornaments.
   ADJECTIVE

2. Upcyle old _____ — Even worn out stuff in your
                 PLURAL NOUN
house can be transformed into _____ décor. Need an Elf
                                       ADJECTIVE
for your shelf? Slap a(n) _____ hat on a(n)
                                 ADJECTIVE
_____ doll and move that thing around every night!
   ADJECTIVE

3. Make your own greeting cards — Try drawing your own! Or,

make your _____ kids do it! Your homemade cards might
               ADJECTIVE
look a bit _____, but your friends and family will still
               ADJECTIVE
_____ them.
   VERB

4. Get back to nature — Nothing says "_____!" like a
                                              EXCLAMATION
door wreath made with _____ from your own yard.
                             NOUN

5. Tree-cycle your paper — Dress up your tree with paper-chain

garlands. Just grab some used paper and scissors and start

_____! To make long enough chains, you'll need about
VERB ENDING IN "ING"

_____ paper strips and _____ glue sticks.
   NUMBER   NUMBER

From *Laugh Your Blank Off! Christmas Edition* ©2022, JBC Story Press

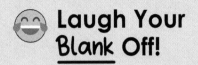

Laugh Your Blank Off!

The One With the Mistletoe

NAME OF FRIEND
ADJECTIVE
ADJECTIVE
ANIMAL
VERB (PAST TENSE)
ADJECTIVE
CHRISTMAS SONG
CHRISTMAS SONG
VERB ENDING IN "ING"
BEVERAGE
VERB ENDING IN "ING"
ADJECTIVE
ADJECTIVE
BODY PART (PLURAL)
VERB
NOUN
EXCLAMATION
BODY PART
EXCLAMATION
VERB ENDING IN "ING"
ADJECTIVE

From *Laugh Your Blank Off! Christmas Edition* ©2022, JBC Story Press

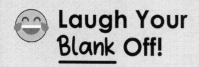

Laugh Your Blank Off!

The One With the Mistletoe

The scene was perfect. We were all at _____'s
                                        NAME OF FRIEND

"_____ Christmas Sweater" party. My sweater had a
 ADJECTIVE

picture of my _____ cat, with the caption, "Meowy
                ADJECTIVE

Catmas." My crush was wearing a sweater with Rudolf the Red-

Nosed _____ on it. The lights twinkled as we
        ANIMAL

_____ and danced to _____ Christmas music,
VERB (PAST TENSE)   ADJECTIVE

like _____ and _____. We took a break from
     CHRISTMAS SONG   CHRISTMAS SONG

_____ and s/he got us some spiked _____.
VERB ENDING IN "ING"   BEVERAGE

But I was so nervous I wasn't sipping as much as _____
                                                  VERB ENDING IN "ING"

my drink. In no time, I was feeling pretty _____ and
                                             ADJECTIVE

wobbly. "_____!" s/he said, looking up, "they hung some
          ADJECTIVE

mistletoe." And then s/he gazed into my _____ and I
                                          BODY PART (PLURAL)

thought I was going to _____. S/he leaned in for a
                         VERB

_____ just as my cup slipped from my hand. I said
  NOUN

"_____!" and bent down to pick it up. Which is how I
  EXCLAMATION

_____-butted her/him right in the face. "_____!
  BODY PART   EXCLAMATION

I'm so sorry!" I said. To my surprise, s/he started _____
                                                     VERB ENDING IN "ING"

and pointing to her/his _____ nose. "Now, I look like my
                         ADJECTIVE

sweater!"

From *Laugh Your Blank Off! Christmas Edition* ©2022, JBC Story Press

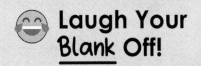 # Laugh Your Blank Off!

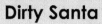 ## Dirty Santa

ADJECTIVE
ANIMAL
VERB
VERB ENDING IN "ING"
ADJECTIVE
VERB
NAME OF FRIEND 1
NOUN
ADJECTIVE
NOUN
NAME OF FRIEND 2
BEVERAGE
BODY PART
NUMBER
ADJECTIVE
ADJECTIVE
BEVERAGE
PLURAL NOUN

From *Laugh Your Blank Off! Christmas Edition* ©2022, JBC Story Press

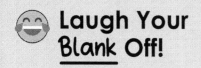 # Laugh Your Blank Off!

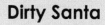 **Dirty Santa**

As fans of gift exchange games will tell you, nothing says Christmas spirit quite like stealing! It's all in _____ fun, of

ADJECTIVE

course. At work, we call it a White _____ gift exchange.

ANIMAL

My book club calls it a Yankee _____. But where I come

VERB

from, we call it Dirty Santa, and _____ is strongly

VERB ENDING IN "ING"

encouraged. Each guest brings a wrapped gift — the funnier and more _____ the gift, the better! After the first gift is

ADJECTIVE

opened, the next person decides if they want to _____ a

VERB

gift from the pile or "steal" an opened gift. One year,

_____ brought down the _____ when her/his gift

NAME OF FRIEND 1   NOUN

was opened. It was a(n) _____ _____!

ADJECTIVE   NOUN

_____ laughed so hard that _____ came out of

NAME OF FRIEND 2   BEVERAGE

her/his _____. Some groups like to limit the number of

BODY PART

times a gift can be stolen to something like _____. To

NUMBER

encourage _____ gift ideas, you could give a prize to the

ADJECTIVE

person whose gift is stolen the most. If you're playing with a(n)

_____ group of "grownups," a big bottle of _____

ADJECTIVE   BEVERAGE

makes a great prize. Try making up your own _____ —

PLURAL NOUN

the dirtier, the better!

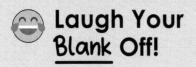
Laugh Your Blank Off!

Unleash the Elf

ADJECTIVE
VERB
VERB
PLURAL NOUN
ADJECTIVE
ANIMAL
NOUN
ADJECTIVE
VERB
NOUN
VERB
FOOD
VERB
NOUN
ADJECTIVE
ADJECTIVE

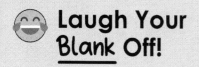

Laugh Your Blank Off!

Unleash the Elf

Have the kids been asking when the The Elf is coming back, but you're fresh out of _____ (ADJECTIVE) ideas for elf stunts? Don't _____ (VERB)! Here are some elf-tastic ideas that will make your family _____ (VERB).

1. Fishing—With a peppermint stick and some string, your elf can fish for _____ (PLURAL NOUN) in the toilet.

2. Rub-a-Dub-Dubbing—Fill a sink with marshmallows and let your elf take a(n) _____ (ADJECTIVE) bath with his/her favorite rubber _____ (ANIMAL).

3. Cheering—Attach your elf to the ceiling fan with a note that says "I'm your biggest _____ (NOUN)."

4. Climbing—Use _____ (ADJECTIVE) star bows to make a climbing wall and have your elf _____ (VERB) to new heights.

5. Chilling—Wrap your elf in a _____ (NOUN) to keep her/him cozy and _____ (VERB) him in the fridge. Then ask your kid to get the milk out (tee hee).

6. Cooking—Put some mini _____ (FOOD) on a toothpick and let your elf _____ (VERB) them over a _____ (NOUN)-powered candle. The possibilities are endless! Just don't forget to move your _____ (ADJECTIVE) elf or you might end up on The _____ (ADJECTIVE) List!

From *Laugh Your Blank Off! Christmas Edition* ©2022, JBC Story Press

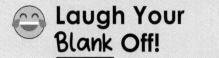

Laugh Your Blank Off!

Holiday Spirits

PLURAL NOUN
ADJECTIVE
VERB ENDING IN "ING"
ADJECTIVE
ADJECTIVE
ADJECTIVE
ADJECTIVE
ADJECTIVE
FOOD
ADJECTIVE
FOOD
VERB
ADJECTIVE
ADJECTIVE
EXCLAMATION
ADJECTIVE
ADJECTIVE
ADJECTIVE
VERB

From *Laugh Your Blank Off! Christmas Edition* ©2022, JBC Story Press

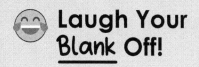

Holiday Spirits

Are you entertaining _____ over the holidays and want
                                     PLURAL NOUN
everyone's spirits to be merry and _____? Special seasonal
                                                ADJECTIVE
cocktails are perfect for _____ with friends. Not only do they
                                   VERB ENDING IN "ING"
taste _____, but they're also fun to make! Christmas is the
          ADJECTIVE
_____ time to practice your mixology skills. So, here are
   ADJECTIVE
some _____ ideas you can try:
        ADJECTIVE

A(n) _____ apple cider hits all the cozy notes.
      ADJECTIVE

For a mix of sweet and tart and spicy, try _____ Sangria.
                                                   ADJECTIVE

A _____ Daiquiri offers a light yet bold sip.
   FOOD

A(n) _____ White Russian is the perfect nightcap next to the
      ADJECTIVE
fire.

For dessert lovers, whip up a Caramel _____ Martini or a
                                              FOOD
spiked Peppermint Milkshake. Or _____ your shake without
                                       VERB
the alcohol. That's called a "Bah Humbug" – but it's _____
                                                                          ADJECTIVE
for designated sleigh drivers! Be sure to serve your creative cocktails

in _____ drinkware to really make your guests say
   ADJECTIVE
"_____!" Whether you're craving something sweet,
 EXCLAMATION
_____, cold, _____, fruity, _____, or spicy,
  ADJECTIVE   ADJECTIVE   ADJECTIVE
these festive drink recipes will raise spirits high. To keep spirits from

getting too high (and having guests _____ on your couch),
                                                 VERB
serve lots of tasty snacks too.

From *Laugh Your Blank Off! Christmas Edition* ©2022, JBC Story Press

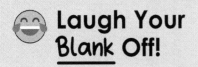

Laugh Your Blank Off!

Office Christmas Party

ADJECTIVE
VERB ENDING IN "ING"
VERB ENDING IN "ING"
PLURAL NOUN
ADJECTIVE
VERB (PAST TENSE)
ADJECTIVE
FOOD
ADJECTIVE
BEVERAGE
NUMBER
NOUN
ADJECTIVE
BODY PART (PLURAL)
NOUN
NOUN
ADJECTIVE
CHRISTMAS SONG
EXCLAMATION

From *Laugh Your Blank Off! Christmas Edition* ©2022, JBC Story Press

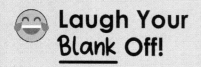

Office Christmas Party

Our company's employees are known for going above and beyond. Which is _____ (ADJECTIVE)! Unless you're talking about _____ (VERB ENDING IN "ING") and _____ (VERB ENDING IN "ING") during the office holiday party. My coworkers love _____ (PLURAL NOUN) almost as much as they love meetings! (Haha – just a little _____ (ADJECTIVE) humor there). The company _____ (VERB (PAST TENSE)) a(n) _____ (ADJECTIVE) band and a fantastic chef who created amazing dishes, including platters of grilled _____ (FOOD) and _____ (ADJECTIVE) desserts. There was even an ice luge for drinking chilled shots of _____ (BEVERAGE)! Out of the _____ (NUMBER) bad decisions made that night, that was about the third worst. The second was holding the party in the company's _____ (NOUN). _____ (ADJECTIVE) employees photocopied their _____ (BODY PART (PLURAL)), broke into the office of the Chief _____ (NOUN) Officer, and left the copies everywhere. Someone took a picture of the CEO's wife kissing a(n) _____ (NOUN) and posted it on social media. But maybe the #1 worst decision was hiring _____ (ADJECTIVE) entertainers to perform. We loved it when they started singing _____ (CHRISTMAS SONG), but when Mr. and Mrs. Claus started taking off their red robes… _____ (EXCLAMATION)!

From *Laugh Your Blank Off! Christmas Edition* ©2022, JBC Story Press

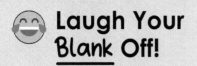

Laugh Your Blank Off!

Holiday Bake-Off

FIRST NAME, LAST NAME OF FRIEND 1
FIRST NAME, LAST NAME OF FRIEND 2
PLACE
CLOTHING ITEM (PLURAL)
ADJECTIVE
NOUN
NOUN
ADJECTIVE
LIQUID
NUMBER
FOOD
FOOD
FOOD
PLURAL NOUN
NOUN
NOUN
ADJECTIVE
VERB (PAST TENSE)
EXCLAMATION
NOUN

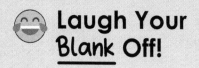

Laugh Your Blank Off!

Holiday Bake-Off

This is _____ reporting live on YNN with
      FIRST NAME, LAST NAME OF FRIEND 1

some lighter news. Earlier today, _____, a
                                    FIRST NAME, LAST NAME OF FRIEND 2

local woman/man from _____ won the National
                          PLACE

Gingerbread House Baking Championship! This talented baking

fan blew the _____ off judges with her/his _____
              CLOTHING ITEM (PLURAL)   ADJECTIVE

entry, which s/he named "My Sweet Dream _____." This
                                             NOUN

winning creation was more of a _____ than a house,
                                   NOUN

complete with _____ TVs, a pool filled with
                ADJECTIVE

_____, and a _____-car garage, all crafted from
   LIQUID   NUMBER

colorful _____, _____, and sprinkles of
           FOOD   FOOD

_____. As you can see behind me, there is a long line of
   FOOD

_____ waiting for their turn to take a selfie with the winning
 PLURAL NOUN

creation. People love pretending that they're about to take a huge

_____ of the gingerbread house. Surprisingly, this is the
   NOUN

first baking _____ this year's winner has ever entered.
                NOUN

Which makes it even more _____ that she/he
                             ADJECTIVE

_____ the long-time defending champion of this popular
VERB (PAST TENSE)

competition. When asked how s/he would celebrate this sweet

victory, the newly crowned champ said, "_____! I'm going
                                          EXCLAMATION

to _____ World!"
      NOUN

From *Laugh Your Blank Off! Christmas Edition* ©2022, JBC Story Press

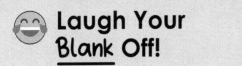
Laugh Your Blank Off!

Eat, Drink and Be Merry

ADJECTIVE
ADJECTIVE
NOUN
CLOTHING ITEM (PLURAL)
CLOTHING ITEM (PLURAL)
FORM OF TRANSPORTATION
ADJECTIVE
NOUN
PLURAL NOUN
ADVERB ENDING IN "LY"
BODY PART (PLURAL)
NOUN
ADJECTIVE
ADJECTIVE
OCCUPATION (PLURAL)
CLOTHING ITEM (PLURAL)
PLURAL NOUN
VERB (PAST TENSE)
SILLY SOUND
EXCLAMATION

From *Laugh Your Blank Off! Christmas Edition* ©2022, JBC Story Press

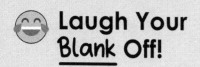

Eat, Drink and Be Merry

One drink, two drinks, three drinks… FLOOR. That's the short version of our _____ Girls Night Out. Now here's the
ADJECTIVE

longer one. Last December, our boyfriends and husbands went on a(n) _____ trip, so we decided to plan our own
ADJECTIVE

_____. We dressed in cute red _____ and
NOUN   CLOTHING ITEM (PLURAL)

_____ with loads of sequins! We took a(n) _____
CLOTHING ITEM (PLURAL)   FORM OF TRANSPORTATION

and went downtown to a club called The _____
                                                    ADJECTIVE

_____. We drank festive _____, sang Christmas
NOUN   PLURAL NOUN

songs way too _____, and danced our _____ off!
              ADVERB ENDING IN "LY"   BODY PART (PLURAL)

We should have ordered some _____ to go with the
                                   NOUN

_____ drinks we were having to keep us from getting too
ADJECTIVE

_____. But we were too busy flirting with gorgeous
ADJECTIVE

_____ dressed in Santa _____ and taking
OCCUPATION (PLURAL)   CLOTHING ITEM (PLURAL)

_____ of each other. We even joined a huge bachelor
PLURAL NOUN

party for a while. Safely back home again, we _____
                                                VERB (PAST TENSE)

each other to secrecy and were about to go to sleep when

suddenly our phones started going "_____" with
                                        SILLY SOUND

notifications. "Oh, _____!" I said when I looked at my
                      EXCLAMATION

phone. Did one of you post something?!

From *Laugh Your Blank Off! Christmas Edition* ©2022, JBC Story Press

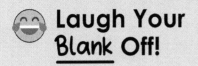

Reindeer Games

VERB
ADJECTIVE
VERB
COLOR
NOUN
ADJECTIVE
PLURAL NOUN
ADJECTIVE
VERB
ADJECTIVE
ANIMAL
ADJECTIVE
ADVERB ENDING IN "LY"
NOUN
FOOD
VERB

From *Laugh Your Blank Off! Christmas Edition* ©2022, JBC Story Press

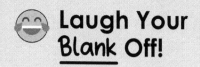

Laugh Your Blank Off!

Reindeer Games

The holidays are the best time of year to _____ and have
                                              VERB
fun with family and friends. This year, add more cheering to your

holiday cheer time with these _____ "Reindeer Games."
                                ADJECTIVE

Everyone gets to _____, of course! Even your
                      VERB

_____-nosed friends!
  COLOR

1. Name That _____ – This game will make you FA LA LA
                  NOUN

LA laugh out loud! See who can guess _____ Christmas
                                         ADJECTIVE

songs the fastest after hearing only a few _____.
                                              PLURAL NOUN

2. Two Truths and a Lie – Each player shares three of their

_____ Christmas traditions. The goal is for others to
  ADJECTIVE

_____ which of them is a lie. Don't worry! Santa won't put
  VERB

you on the _____ List for lying.
              ADJECTIVE

3. Pin the Tail on the _____ – This classic party game is
                           ANIMAL

even more _____ if guests are enjoying adult beverages.
              ADJECTIVE

Tipsy friends may miss the mark so _____ that they end
                                       ADVERB ENDING IN "LY"

up in another room!

4. Holiday Bake-Off – Turn up the _____ at your party
                                       NOUN

with a little fun competition! Ask your guests to bring a homemade

_____ and then vote for the winner. Bonus for party
  FOOD

hosts: You don't have to _____ dessert!
                              VERB

From *Laugh Your Blank Off! Christmas Edition* ©2022, JBC Story Press

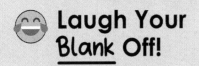

Laugh Your Blank Off!

All I Want for Christmas is True Love

NUMBER
ANIMAL
VERB
ADJECTIVE
ADJECTIVE
PLURAL NOUN
NUMBER
BODY PART (PLURAL)
NUMBER
NOUN
ADJECTIVE
ADJECTIVE
NOUN
PLURAL NOUN
PLACE
NAME OF FRIEND

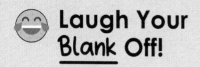

Laugh Your Blank Off!

All I Want for Christmas is True Love

Dear Santa,

This the most important letter I've ever written to you. It's even more important than the one I wrote when I was _____ years old
                                                                                    NUMBER
and asked for a pet _____. All I want for Christmas this
                         ANIMAL
year is to _____ my one true love. I'm not asking for
              VERB
much, and the characteristics I'm looking for in my _____
                                                         ADJECTIVE
partner are pretty _____. I've created a short list of
                       ADJECTIVE
_____ to help guide your search. My soulmate should:
PLURAL NOUN

1. Be at least _____ feet tall.
                NUMBER
2. Have six-pack _____.
                  BODY PART (PLURAL)
3. Earn at least _____ dollars per year (less than that is a
                   NUMBER
definite _____-breaker).
           NOUN
4. Be very _____ and _____. The kind of
            ADJECTIVE   ADJECTIVE
person, for example, who will always remember how I like my

_____.
   NOUN
5. Love going on extravagant _____ to places like
                              PLURAL NOUN
_____ at least once a year.
   PLACE

Thanks, Santa! You're the best!

XOXO,

_____
NAME OF FRIEND

From *Laugh Your Blank Off! Christmas Edition* ©2022, JBC Story Press

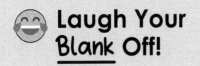

Laugh Your Blank Off!

My Friend the Grinch

NAME OF FRIEND
PLACE
VERB
VERB ENDING IN "ING"
ADJECTIVE
VERB (PAST TENSE)
EXCLAMATION
ADJECTIVE
ADJECTIVE
ADVERB ENDING IN "LY"
ADJECTIVE
SINGER
NUMBER
BEVERAGE
COLOR

From *Laugh Your Blank Off! Christmas Edition* ©2022, JBC Story Press

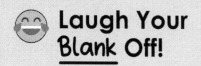

Laugh Your Blank Off!

My Friend the Grinch

I'll never forget the year I brought my friend, _____, home
                                                NAME OF FRIEND

for Christmas. Her/his family lives far away, in _____, so I
                                                  PLACE

decided to invite her/him to celebrate with my family.

S/he is always making our friends _____, so I thought it
                                   VERB

would be fun _____ out for the holidays. Big mistake!
              VERB ENDING IN "ING"

Turns out s/he is not as _____ as I thought. I got my first
                          ADJECTIVE

hint when we _____ through my parents' cheerfully
              VERB (PAST TENSE)

decorated neighborhood. S/he groaned and said "_____!
                                                EXCLAMATION

What is this place, the Town of Who-ville?" Later, when it was time

for dinner, s/he refused to try my mom's _____ ham. I
                                          ADJECTIVE

don't eat "roast beast," s/he grumped. You should have seen the

_____ look on my Mom's face. "Too bad for you," I said
ADJECTIVE

_____, "because we're fresh out of Who Hash." Then,
ADVERB ENDING IN "LY"

later that night, s/he complained about my _____'s holiday
                                            ADJECTIVE

music playlist. S/he said, "If I have to listen to _____
                                                    SINGER

_____ more times I need a lot of booze in this _____."
NUMBER   BEVERAGE

What a grinch! Then again, her/his skin does look a little

_____.
COLOR

From *Laugh Your Blank Off! Christmas Edition* ©2022, JBC Story Press

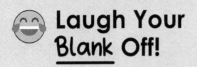

Laugh Your Blank Off!

Not Your Grandma's Eggnog

VERB
EXCLAMATION
VERB
NUMBER
NUMBER
LIQUID
NUMBER
VERB (PAST TENSE)
FOOD
VERB
ADJECTIVE
VERB ENDING IN "ING"
BODY PART
ADJECTIVE
ADVERB ENDING IN "LY"
PLURAL NOUN
ADJECTIVE
NOUN
VERB
NUMBER
ADVERB ENDING IN "LY"

From *Laugh Your Blank Off! Christmas Edition* ©2022, JBC Story Press

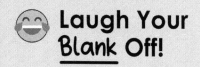

Laugh Your Blank Off!

Not Your Grandma's Eggnog

This holiday season, _____ your party guests with a
                         VERB
creative twist on a holiday classic. One sip of "Not Your Grandma's
Eggnog," and your guests will say, "_____!" That's
                                      EXCLAMATION
delicious!" Thanks to a very special ingredient, this eggnog will
become your new favorite. Just don't _____ Grandma!
                                          VERB
You'll need: _____ egg(s), one cup of sugar, _____ cup(s) of
              NUMBER   NUMBER
whiskey, three cups of _____, _____ cup(s) of milk, ½
                          LIQUID   NUMBER
teaspoon freshly _____ nutmeg. And… the secret
                 VERB (PAST TENSE)
ingredient, _____! Blend it until it's smooth.
                 FOOD
Step 1: _____ the eggs and sugar until they are
           VERB
_____. Step 2: Add the milk then start _____
  ADJECTIVE   VERB ENDING IN "ING"
until your _____ feels like it is going to fall off. Ask a
            BODY PART
friend to take over until the mixture is nice and _____.
                                                    ADJECTIVE
Step 3: _____ add the liquor and mix thoroughly. Step 4:
         ADVERB ENDING IN "LY"
Pour the nog into _____ and let chill in the fridge – or
                    PLURAL NOUN
outdoors if it's _____! Step 5: When your awesome
                  ADJECTIVE
eggnog is cool enough, garnish with a _____ of nutmeg
                                          NOUN
and _____ it to your guests. Step 6: Enjoy! This recipe
       VERB
makes _____ servings, so remember to drink _____!
       NUMBER   ADVERB ENDING IN "LY"

From *Laugh Your Blank Off! Christmas Edition* ©2022 JBC Story Press

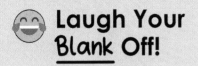

Laugh Your Blank Off!

Staying in My Childhood Room

EMOTION
COLOR
CELEBRITY
CELEBRITY
NOUN
NOUN
ADJECTIVE
VERB (PAST TENSE)
PLURAL NOUN
COLOR
NOUN
NOUN
ADJECTIVE
ADJECTIVE
VERB (PAST TENSE)
VERB
ADJECTIVE
PLURAL NOUN
BODY PART
PLURAL NOUN
EXCLAMATION

From *Laugh Your Blank Off! Christmas Edition* ©2022, JBC Story Press

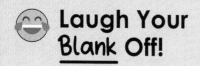

Laugh Your Blank Off!

Staying in My Childhood Room

I'll never forget bringing my boyfriend home with me for the holidays the first time. I was so _____ (EMOTION) to show him my childhood bedroom. The walls are painted hot _____ (COLOR) and covered in posters of _____ (CELEBRITY) and _____ (CELEBRITY) from Teen _____ (NOUN) magazine. A disco _____ (NOUN) hangs from the ceiling, and my _____ (ADJECTIVE) boombox sits on the dresser that I _____ (VERB PAST TENSE) myself, with little _____ (PLURAL NOUN) all over it. My neon _____ (COLOR) comforter clashes with the color of the walls. And, of course, there is a lava _____ (NOUN) next to my bed. When I left for college, my parents turned my bedroom into a home _____ (NOUN). So, now there is a(n) _____ (ADJECTIVE) treadmill and _____ (ADJECTIVE) balls _____ (VERB PAST TENSE) in the room. At night, we did our best to _____ (VERB) through the night on the _____ (ADJECTIVE) bed. I love snuggling, but we were packed in like _____ (PLURAL NOUN). In the morning, we would wake up with the worst case of "bed-_____ (BODY PART)" you have ever seen. My parents kept adding gym _____ (PLURAL NOUN) to my old room, so the next year, we just booked a hotel room. _____ (EXCLAMATION)! So much better!

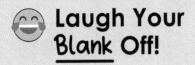
Laugh Your Blank Off!

Not-So-Humble Holiday Brag

EMOTION
ADJECTIVE
ADJECTIVE
EXCLAMATION
NUMBER
PLACE
VERB ENDING IN "ING"
VERB
NUMBER
NAME OF FRIEND
EMOTION
EXCLAMATION
NOUN
NAME OF FRIEND
PLACE
ADJECTIVE
ADJECTIVE
PLURAL NOUN
VERB
PLACE

From *Laugh Your Blank Off! Christmas Edition* ©2022, JBC Story Press

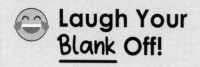

Not-So-Humble Holiday Brag

Dear Friends,

Merry Christmas! We are so _____ to share the
                              EMOTION

_____ things that happened this year. We bought a(n)
  ADJECTIVE

_____ vacation home. You're probably thinking,
  ADJECTIVE

"_____! Another one?!" That's right! We now have
   EXCLAMATION

_____ in all. This one is in _____, which is known for its
 NUMBER   PLACE

awesome _____. We hope you will visit us there! Just be
         VERB ENDING IN "ING"

sure to _____ far in advance *wink wink.* We only have
          VERB

_____ guest rooms. _____ Jr. graduated from
 NUMBER   NAME OF FRIEND

medical school! We are so _____ that he wants to be a
                             EMOTION

doctor. _____! He's going to make so much
         EXCLAMATION

_____! We celebrated _____'s wedding in
   NOUN   NAME OF FRIEND

_____. The ceremony was amazing and the reception
   PLACE

was as _____ as you would expect from us. The
         ADJECTIVE

_____ couple made their grand entrance riding on
   ADJECTIVE

_____! We were so disappointed that some of you were
  PLURAL NOUN

not able to _____. So, you're all invited to celebrate their
              VERB

first anniversary at our vacation home in _____. We wish
                                              PLACE

you all a joyous holiday season and a new year as prosperous as

ours!

XOXO

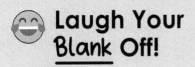
Laugh Your Blank Off!

Christmas in July

VERB
PLURAL NOUN
PLURAL NOUN
NUMBER
PLACE
PLURAL NOUN
FOOD
CLOTHING ITEM (PLURAL)
ADJECTIVE
PLURAL NOUN
PLURAL NOUN
NOUN
PLURAL NOUN
BEVERAGE
NOUN
PLURAL NOUN
NOUN
VERB
ADJECTIVE
EXCLAMATION

From *Laugh Your Blank Off! Christmas Edition* ©2022, JBC Story Press

Laugh Your Blank Off!

Christmas in July

When it comes to celebrating Christmas, once a year is just not enough! My extended family _____ Christmas so much
                                            VERB

that we deck the _____ and exchange _____ in
                PLURAL NOUN   PLURAL NOUN

December *and* July, or "Jolly July" as we call it. All _____
                                                                           NUMBER

of us head to the beautiful beaches of _____. We string
                                                      PLACE

_____ on the beach house, make peppermint
PLURAL NOUN

_____, wear Christmas-themed _____ and build
   FOOD   CLOTHING ITEM (PLURAL)

_____ sandmen by the ocean. We collect _____,
 ADJECTIVE   PLURAL NOUN

go fishing, feast on delicious food, and play lots of _____.
                                                                 PLURAL NOUN

Instead of dashing through the snow, we race across the

_____ on jet skis. The night before we open
  NOUN

_____, we leave out cold _____ and cookies for
PLURAL NOUN   BEVERAGE

Santa Claus next to the Christmas cactus. They're always gone in

the morning! Although Santa does leave a trail of _____
                                                                 NOUN

behind. Wonder if he's wearing _____ or flipflops? Every
                                   PLURAL NOUN

year, someone receives a new _____ that we can play
                                    NOUN

outside. So we all _____ to the beach and crank up the
                    VERB

holiday music. Some people give us _____ looks, but
                                        ADJECTIVE

others wish us "_____ Christmas!"
                  EXCLAMATION

From *Laugh Your Blank Off! Christmas Edition* ©2022, JBC Story Press

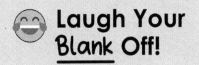

Laugh Your Blank Off!

Christmas Karaoke Night

EXCLAMATION
ADJECTIVE
NOUN
NAME OF FRIEND
ADVERB ENDING IN "LY"
NOUN
ADJECTIVE
ADJECTIVE
BEVERAGE
SINGER
ADJECTIVE
ADJECTIVE
ADJECTIVE
ADJECTIVE
VERB
CHRISTMAS SONG
ADJECTIVE
NUMBER
BEVERAGE

From *Laugh Your Blank Off! Christmas Edition* ©2022, JBC Story Press

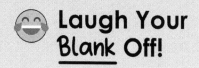

Laugh Your Blank Off!

Christmas Karaoke Night

I can still hear my friends cheering me on. "_____!" they
                                              EXCLAMATION
shouted. "You've got this!" My favorite memory last holiday season

was the night we went to the _____ _____ Bar
                              ADJECTIVE NOUN

for Christmas Karaoke. At first, I did NOT want to go. But my

friend, _____, _____ forced me to. S/he knows I
        NAME OF FRIEND ADVERB ENDING IN "LY"

love to sing in the _____, but I get _____ about
                     NOUN   ADJECTIVE

singing in public. S/he said it would be a(n) _____ chance
                                              ADJECTIVE

to practice and, after having some _____, I would feel
                                   BEVERAGE

ready to sing like _____. I was still really _____,
                   SINGER   ADJECTIVE

so s/he also mentioned that they were giving out cash prizes to

the _____ performers of the night. That was the last bit of
    ADJECTIVE

motivation I needed. The singers were really _____ so I
                                             ADJECTIVE

started to get _____ again. I tried to _____, but
               ADJECTIVE   VERB

my friends would not let me off the hook. When it was my turn, I

belted out my all-time favorite Christmas song, _____.
                                                CHRISTMAS SONG

The crowd went _____! And I couldn't believe it, but I won
                ADJECTIVE

_____ dollars! To celebrate, I bought _____
NUMBER   BEVERAGE

shots for everyone in the bar. What a night!

From *Laugh Your Blank Off! Christmas Edition* ©2022, JBC Story Press

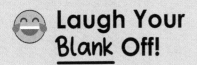

Laugh Your Blank Off!

'Twas the Night Before Christmas

NOUN
NOUN
PLURAL NOUN
VERB (PAST TENSE)
NOUN
VERB (PAST TENSE)
BODY PART (PLURAL)
ADJECTIVE
NUMBER
NOUN
ADJECTIVE
NOUN
VERB (PAST TENSE)
VERB ENDING IN "ING"
VERB ENDING IN "ING"
VERB (PAST TENSE)
ADJECTIVE
ADJECTIVE

From *Laugh Your Blank Off! Christmas Edition* ©2022, JBC Story Press

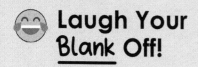

Laugh Your Blank Off!

'Twas the Night Before Christmas

'Twas the night before Christmas, when all through the house,

Not a _____ was stirring, not even a mouse;
      NOUN

The stockings were hung by the _____ with care,
                                      NOUN

In hopes that St. Nicholas soon would be there;

The _____ were nestled all snug in their beds,
    PLURAL NOUN

While visions of sugar plums _____ in their heads,
                             VERB (PAST TENSE)

When out on the _____ there arose such a clatter,
                      NOUN

I _____ from the bed to see what was the matter.
  VERB (PAST TENSE)

When, what to my wondering _____ should appear,
                          BODY PART (PLURAL)

But a(n) _____ sleigh, and _____ reindeer,
        ADJECTIVE   NUMBER

Down the chimney St. Nicholas came with a whack,

A _____ of toys was flung on his back,
   NOUN

He was _____ and plump, a right jolly old elf,
      ADJECTIVE

He spoke not a _____, but went straight to his work,
           NOUN

And filled all the stockings; then _____ with a jerk,
                           VERB (PAST TENSE)

And _____ his finger aside of his nose,
   VERB ENDING IN "ING"

And _____ a nod, up the chimney he rose.
   VERB ENDING IN "ING"

But I heard him exclaim, before he _____ out of sight,
                                  VERB (PAST TENSE)

_____ Christmas to all, and to all a(n) _____
  ADJECTIVE   ADJECTIVE

good night!

From *Laugh Your Blank Off! Christmas Edition* ©2022 JBC Story Press

Thank you for trying us out

A favor please

Would you take a quick minute to leave us a rating/review on Amazon? It makes a *HUGE* difference and we would really appreciate it!

JBC Story Press

 Do you like freebies?
Please send email to
info@jbcempowerpress.com
and we'll send you free funny stuff!

Made in the USA
Las Vegas, NV
19 December 2024